Maggie Walker

Business Leader

Written by Garnet Nelson Jackson

Illustrated by Keaf Holliday

MODERN CURRICULUM PRESS

Program Reviewers

Leila Eames, Coordinator of Instruction,
    Chapter 1
    New Orleans Public Schools
    New Orleans, Louisiana

Stephanie Mahan, Teacher
    Bethune Elementary School
    San Diego, California

Thomasina M. Portis, Director
    Multicultural/Values Education
    District of Columbia
        Public Schools
    Washington, D.C.

MODERN CURRICULUM PRESS

13900 Prospect Road, Cleveland, Ohio 44136

A Paramount Publishing Company

ISBN 0-8136-5242-1 (Reinforced Binding)   0-8136-5248-0 (Paperback)

Library of Congress Catalog Card Number: 93-79424

Dear Readers,

When Maggie Walker was young, she was very poor. But she changed that by working hard in school. Years later, she became the president of a bank.

Maggie wanted to help people— especially boys and girls. She did not want them to be poor as she had been. She showed them ways for improving their lives.

Like Maggie, we should help others besides ourselves. We should always try to help those in need.

Your friend,

Garnet Jackson

When she was very young,
Maggie spent many hours playing
in the garden. She loved the
flowers. Sometimes she would
sing with the birds.

1

Years before, Maggie's parents had
been forced to work as slaves. Now,
in 1870, they were free. They worked
for the Van Lew family and lived in
their house. When Maggie wasn't
playing in the garden, she was
reading her school books.

3

When Maggie was ten years old, her stepfather died. Maggie and her family moved to Richmond, Virginia. She helped her mother wash other people's clothes to make money.

Maggie grew up to be the smartest in her high school class. She was very good at reading and working with numbers. Maggie graduated when she was sixteen. Then Maggie taught in the public school for a few years.

When Maggie was about 19 years old, she met Armistead Walker. They fell in love, married, and later had two sons, Melvin and Russell.

Maggie went to work for a group called the Independent Order of St. Luke. This group gave African Americans business advice. They also cared for the sick and elderly.

After a few years, Maggie was directing much of the work at the Order of St. Luke. Maggie had lots of energy and was very good at her job.

One day Maggie thought of a new idea. She would give people a place to save their money. In 1903, she founded the St. Luke Penny Savings Bank and became its president.

Maggie was the first woman bank president in the United States.

Many people were very excited about Maggie's bank. The bank and the Order of St. Luke grew larger and larger.

Later, Maggie started a newspaper called the *St. Luke Herald*. Many enjoyed reading this paper to find out what was happening at the bank.

Along with caring for her family, Maggie worked very hard at the bank. Maggie's bank helped many African Americans start businesses and buy homes. It became one of the biggest in Richmond, Virginia.

14

15

Maggie loved children. She
remembered what it was like to be
poor. Maggie talked to the children
in schools about saving their pennies.
She even gave them little boxes to
put their money in.

Maggie spent a lot of time raising money for the sick and poor people in Richmond. In 1912, she founded a home for African American girls who needed a place to stay.

Maggie joined groups that tried to make Richmond a better place to live. She wanted all children to be healthy and educated. She wanted all women and men to be able to find jobs.

Maggie Lena Walker was known for her hard work and for helping others. In 1934, just two months before she died, Maggie was given a special honor. That year, the month of October was set aside as "Maggie Lena Walker Month" in the state of Virginia. Small statues of her were put in schools and businesses.

Maggie Lena Walker

Before Maggie Walker—
And this is no tale—
Bank presidents in America
Had always been male.

She started her bank
For all to see
In Richmond, Virginia,
In 1903.

24

To help American children
Have a better life,
She began a school fund,
And lessened their strife.

She started a home
For American girls,
To help them solve problems
And succeed in their world.

People loved Maggie Walker.
Many knew her by name.
With statues she was honored.
This lady had earned her fame.

Glossary

bank (baŋk) A place where people save money

found (foʊ nd) Begin something

honor (än´ ər) To show that you think someone is important and good

member (mem´ bər) Someone who belongs to a group

president (prez´ i dənt) The person in charge of a group

slave (slāv) A person who is owned by someone else, and must do whatever the owner wants

statue (stach´ o͞o) An object made to look like a person